Never
Give Up

LEGACY
p r e s s

Published by Legacy Press

Copyright © 2020 by Kevin Barker and Melissa Morse

For permission, please write to Kevin Barker:
barkmank@gmail.com

Printed in the United States of America

Library of Congress Control Number:

ISBN (softcover): 978-1-7342435-2-9

ISBN (ebook): 978-1-7342435-3-6

Available from Amazon.com and other retail outlets.

Names of individuals living at the time of publication are used with permission.

Ghostwritten by Robin Grunder, LegacyPress.org

Edited by Kendall Emmert, KendallEmmert.com

Publishing Consultant: Renee Fisher, ReneeFisher.com

Cover design, interior layout by Nelly Murariu, PixBeeDesign.com

Never Give Up

A FATHER'S PURSUIT OF
HIS CHILD'S HEART

♥

Kevin Barker & Melissa Morse
with Robin Grunder

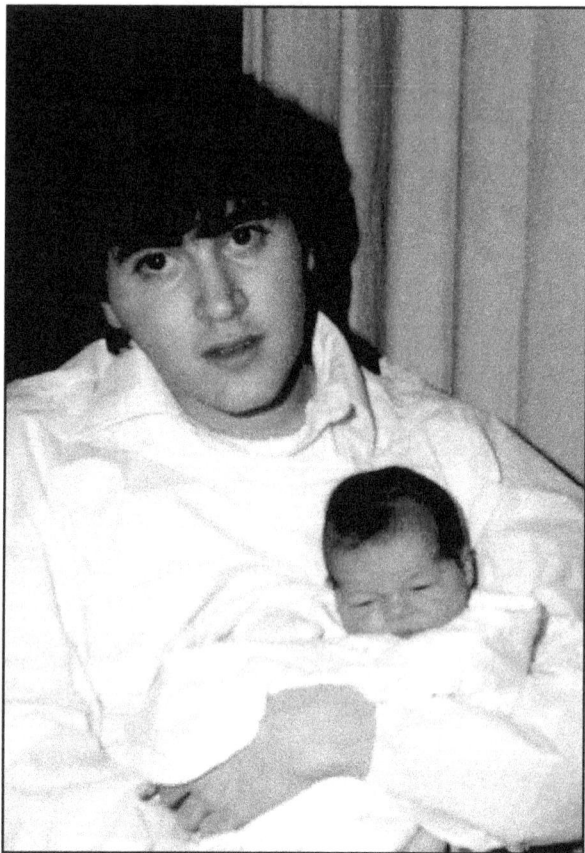

MY LIFESAVER

TABLE OF CONTENTS

Acknowledgements

First and foremost, I dedicate the words on these pages and the story of my life to my Lord Jesus Christ. I would have nothing and be nothing if it were not for His saving grace. He has never given up on me no matter what I have done. He has loved me just as He promises in his word.

Secondly, I dedicate this book to my children Melissa and Bradley.

To my daughter, Melissa, who helped me fill in the gaps on these pages. I had no idea the true gift you were for so long. Though your entrance into this world was not planned by me, your Creator planned and knew about you before time began. I believe God sent you to me and that you saved my life. I am so proud of you in so many ways. You are daddy's little princess. I love you, sweetheart.

To my son, Bradley. You are an amazing dad and husband. You far exceed me as a father. Your selfless love continues to inspire me. May you always know that I believe in you and that you can do anything God calls you to. I love you, son.

To my father, a man of few words who would always listen to my endless chatter. I know you "got me" before I even understood myself. I thank God for the 14 years he gave you to me. You never gave up on anything important. I love and miss you.

To my mom who was always relentless about family. You have inspired me in many ways. You were one of the hardest workers I have ever known. You taught me the value of hospitality and that there is always room for one more at our table. I love you, mom.

To our writer, Robin. We could have never completed this book without you. I knew several years ago when we met at a writers' event God wanted me to ask for your help in writing. You have listened to my heart and put those thoughts in writing. I am forever grateful to you. You are a blessing to many.

Kevin Barker

Rusty Boruff

Amazon Best Selling Author of Cell 121 and 12:2
Founder, One-eighty

one)eighty
PREVENT. REACH. DEVELOP.

I highly recommend this book by Kevin and his daughter, Melissa. One, because you can see Kevin's awesome mustache (be sure to not skim over the photos!). But mostly, this is a story that captivates your heart and attention. Kevin shares both the beauty of an honest, broken heart, and an authentic desire to connect with his daughter. The corresponding notes from Melissa illustrate a pain that is so real you can feel it. Yet, both of them were open to allowing God to do what He does best and that is to restore relationships. Seeing this first-hand by knowing Kevin personally, and Melissa from a distance, has given me a unique perspective into the authenticity of the story.

*"Trust in the LORD with all your heart and
lean not on your own understanding;
and in all your ways acknowledge him, and
he will make your paths straight."*

Proverbs 3:5-6 (NIV)

CHAPTER ONE

Kevin

"Their days of labor are filled with pain and grief;
even at night their minds cannot rest.
It is all meaningless."

Ecclesiastes 2:23 NLT

———————✕———————

I feel like I've been chasing after things my entire life. I never really thought they were bad things: a better job, more money, more knowledge, meaningful relationships. Who wouldn't want these things? I certainly can't think of anyone.

Even though these quests all seemed worthy, a constant problem existed. In my mission to pursue everything bigger and better, I kept sinking lower and lower. At the time, I couldn't explain why it was happening. One job would lead to a better job, and I still felt a lack of purpose. More money would allow me to buy more things, and those things just piled up with all the other things—right alongside my stack of anger and bitterness. I worked hard to provide for my family, but the distance between me, my wife, and my children only grew. I couldn't figure out where I was going wrong. Did any of it matter anyway? All this chasing and wanting a better life—maybe it was all pointless? I'm pretty sure there is something in the Bible about that.

I've always kind of known about God and I don't recall a time that I didn't believe in His existence. Growing up, we went to church on occasion, but my personal experience with church and religion was mainly about following rules. For the most part, I followed them. I can't honestly say that I found deeper meaning in religion or its rules. I knew what was expected of me, however, so that is what I did.

I lived most of my life doing what I thought was expected of me. I searched for meaning. I wanted to be happy. I continued to chase after what I thought those things looked like, but all I found was hopelessness.

Until I turned 40.

I found myself holding down three part-time jobs. Working to provide for my family and make the ends meet was another example of doing what

I believed was expected of me. Of those three jobs, there was one I was especially drawn to. The people seemed *different*, like they were truly happy. They seemed to have a positive outlook toward the future. They had a sense of purpose.

The atmosphere was competitive, but my co-workers actually enjoyed celebrating one another's accomplishments. I don't mean *celebrate* the way I was used to celebrating. The whole building-each-other-up thing was foreign to me. The entire environment, including the people throughout the company, was positive. Admittedly, I was also drawn to the ridiculous amount of money many of my co-workers were making!

I couldn't quite put my finger on what made them different. It felt good to be around them. One day, a leader at the company came into the office and said, "Good morning, Barker. We prayed for you this morning." I wasn't quite sure how to respond, but I could see that his comment was genuine. After several months, I became confident that a group of people were praying for me, even though I didn't understand why they were.

I wasn't making the kind of money that many of the others in the company were, but I was learning about financial responsibility. I felt a sense of purpose and camaraderie, even though we weren't going out for drinks after work. I felt genuinely cared for as they spent time investing in me, getting to know me, and mentoring me. And not for the purpose of getting ahead. This attitude was foreign to me, both professionally and personally.

The company offered intensive and inspiring training sessions. "Bootcamp Sales Training" was held over a weekend at a hotel and the speaker was well-known in the industry as a record-holding salesman, so we knew it would be a powerful training from someone who knew what he was talking about. I was hoping that I would gain the tools I needed to boost my career, my wealth, and give me purpose. I wanted to move forward and be able to quit my other two jobs. I wanted freedom to provide for my family without financial strain. I wanted freedom with my time. Needless to say, I was hanging my hope on this conference.

At the beginning of the first session, our company leader, Shane, began our training by talking to God. "I'm not sure where you're at on your journey in life, but if you don't mind, we're going to take a minute to pray. I like to stack the deck in my favor." I was intrigued.

I knew Shane and was familiar with him praying before our meetings and trainings. It was no secret that he was a person of faith. His email signature included a verse from the Bible: "Trust in the Lord with all your heart and lean not on your own understanding" (Proverbs 3:5). I thought it must be an important verse if the wildly successful businessman who I aspired to be like included it on all of his correspondence. Whatever he said, I took to heart and it was actually the first Bible verse that I ever looked up on my own.

The conference was probably the best I had been to since starting with the company. Before the end of the final session on Saturday evening, Shane invited us all back Sunday morning for an informal "church" service. It was an invitation, but I could tell he was strongly suggesting we all come. Did I want to go? I wasn't sure that I did. I was sure, however, that this guy had something going on in his life that was better than what was going on in my own. Not only did he have a big house and all kinds of toys, he had a family that he loved, and they loved him. It seemed like he had everything in life that I wanted. So when he said, "If I were you," I decided to listen. I got up the next morning and went to "church" at the hotel.

The pastor who was invited to speak never showed up so Tom, a featured speaker that weekend,

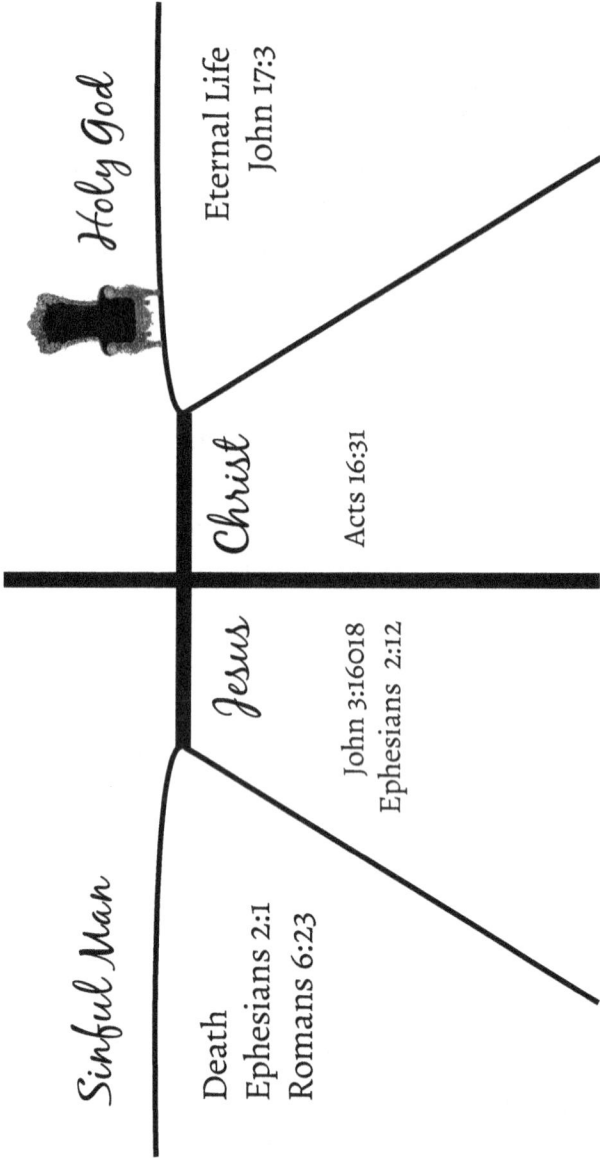

Holy God

Eternal Life
John 17:3

Christ

Acts 16:31

Jesus

John 3:16018
Ephesians 2:12

Sinful Man

Death
Ephesians 2:1
Romans 6:23

ended up leading the service. He was a businessman, not a preacher, so he used an overhead projector and drew a picture. He explained that there was a big divide between us and God. Drawing a cross over that space, he explained that Jesus's life, His death on the cross, and His resurrection was the only bridge between man and God. Nothing else. Nothing we did, worked for, rules we followed . . . nothing could get us to heaven except Jesus.

I wasn't 100 percent sure of what he was talking about, but deep down in my spirit, something started to make sense. All of the sudden, everything that I was striving for and working for, everything I had been chasing after to find purpose and meaning didn't matter. This Jesus that they were talking about wasn't just a story. He was God. And He wanted a relationship with me.

Although Tom invited anyone who wanted to receive the gift of salvation to come up front, I no longer heard his voice. I heard Jesus calling me by name. I couldn't move to the front fast enough. The chains that had been binding my heart were loosening. My mind didn't understand what was happening, but my heart felt light and full at the exact same time. Full of things I had never experienced before: peace, forgiveness, and love.

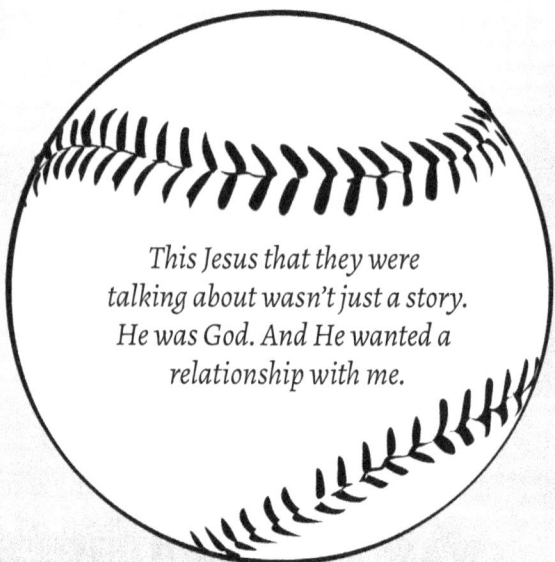

This Jesus that they were talking about wasn't just a story. He was God. And He wanted a relationship with me.

As tears of joy began to fall, the broken pieces of my life that I was clutching began to fall as well; the remnants of shattered dreams, broken relationships, unforgiveness, and feelings of worthlessness dropped. All of the painful shards lay among fragments that were smashed as a result of my own actions and reactions to things and people in my life. I loosened my grasp and laid them at the foot of the cross that day as I accepted Jesus as my Savior.

I wish I could tell you that my pile of pieces and parts were miraculously restored the day I gave my heart over to Christ. That didn't happen. God had a different transformation in mind and, as it turned out, He would ask me to pick up each piece, one by one, and hand them back over to Him.

But there were so many! "God, where do I start?" I cried. The answer was a whisper. My Heavenly Father wanted me to start with my heart and my role as a father. I just hoped that it wasn't too late.

CHAPTER TWO

Melissa

*"If a man owns a hundred sheep, and one of them
wanders away, will he not leave the ninety-nine on
the hills and go to look for the one that wandered
off? And if he finds it, I tell you the truth, he is
happier about that one sheep than about the
ninety-nine that did not wander off."*

Matthew 18:12-13 (NIV)

❤

My dad "found Jesus" when I was twenty years
old. I didn't want anything to do with him.
Jesus or my dad.

I knew who Jesus was. When I was younger, I
attended mass with my grandma on the *"big days."*
Honestly, the most exciting part of church and the
whole Jesus thing was the breakfast we would get
afterwards. I didn't understand any of the words,
prayers, or routines, and no one took the time to

explain them to me. Everything I knew about church felt cold and uninviting. A bunch of rules to follow? No, thank you. I was an adult now. Growing up, I had had enough rules that didn't make sense to last me a lifetime. This Jesus my dad found—dad can keep Him. I'm doing just fine on my own.

I knew who my dad was . . . my controlling, angry, bitter, alcoholic, workaholic dad. My never-around dad. My always-chasing-after-the-next-big-thing dad. When I was in high school and dad didn't think I was abiding by his rules, he literally locked me out of the house. He actually changed the locks on the doors several times. Now, he suddenly wanted to invite me into his life and to be a part of mine? He wanted to build a relationship with me? Talk about a relationship with Jesus? I'm afraid it was too late for all of that. He had locked that door a long time ago too.

I never did drugs. A handful of times I smoked cigarettes and drank. Drinking didn't do much for me and only reminded me of my dad. I masked any pain I was feeling by throwing myself into school, helping my friends as much as I could and, when I was old enough, working crazy hours at K-Mart so that I could be away from the house as much as possible. I had a dire need to do everything the exact opposite of him. I didn't want to grow up to be like the man who I essentially hated and who hated me.

MELISSA WITH HER FATHER.

I intentionally picked fights with my dad. When he came home drunk, I would aggravate him so that he would fight with me. I wanted my dad to get angry with me so that he wouldn't get into it with my mom and brother. I wanted to protect them. I thought if he fought with me long enough, he would get tired and pass out before moving on to one of them. Sometimes it worked.

The relationship between my parents, from what I could tell, was a fragile one. There were many times when I believed my mom was going to leave my dad, and I was all for it. I just wanted the fighting to end. I was never quite sure how or why they stayed together for as long as they did. Maybe it was their mutual desire to have control over every situation they encountered.

It's been about sixteen years since my dad first introduced me to Jesus. Of course, I didn't take it seriously at all. But I was curious. Sometimes I would join my dad in church half-heartedly. Was I waiting for him to fail? For this phase to pass? For him to go back to his old ways? I stuck around long enough to wait and see what would happen, but those doubts were always in the back of my mind.

It took a while, but my heart began to soften. Two years after my dad first introduced the idea of

───────❤───────

*We needed God at the
center of our relationship for there
to be any hope whatsoever.*

───────❤───────

having a relationship with Jesus, I accepted Christ as my Savior and was baptized alongside my wonderful fiancé, Robert. When we started talking about marriage and a future together, I knew enough to realize that we couldn't do this all on our own. We had connected with some couples at church who had solid marriages and wanted our future to be like theirs, not the broken, monotonous, or eggshell-fragile relationships we had seen in both of our parents' marriages. We needed God at the center of our relationship for there to be any hope whatsoever. By the time Robert and I were married, Christ was the foundation of our relationship and the foundation of our lives.

Admittedly, I was grateful that my dad had found Jesus, but I was still skeptical of having a relationship with my earthly father, even though he had introduced me to my Heavenly Father. Sometimes things are just too far gone, too broken to be fixed. Sometimes it's just too late. I had long since given up on a relationship with my dad.

CHAPTER THREE

Kevin

"You can make many plans,
but the LORD's purpose will prevail."

Proverbs 19:21 (NLT)

———————✕———————

When I was kid, I loved my dad. I looked up to him. He commanded respect in our home and got it. That is just how things were done and what was expected. When I was growing up, he was kind of my hero.

Dad didn't have the greatest situation when he was a child. He was barely old enough to remember his parents' divorce. When it came time to decide custody, the judge asked my dad who he wanted to live with. The only thing my dad knew at that time was that his dad wouldn't let him take his toys to his mom's house and he wanted to be able to play with his toys. What six-year-old wouldn't? The decision to grant his mother custody was based off of a six-year-old wanting to play and where his toys were located. The judge should have known better. My dad never saw his father again and his mom changed their name without the knowledge of his father. My dad was never able to track down his father's side of the family, and that heritage is lost to us all. Even now as I write this, it makes me angry that such a huge life decision was placed in the hands of a child.

My grandmother remarried a man with the last name of Barker, and they made their home in the New York City area during the Depression. Times were tough every way you looked at it. In 8th grade, Dad quit school to take care of his brother and sister and help provide for his family. Even with a rough start in life, my dad managed to make something out of it. He met and married my mom, while having a successful career as a Lieutenant of Internal Affairs for the Rock Island Police Department in Illinois. Dad worked hard and provided well for his family.

My mom and dad had two children a decade before I came along. In many ways, I was like an only child. My brother and sister struggled with me and,

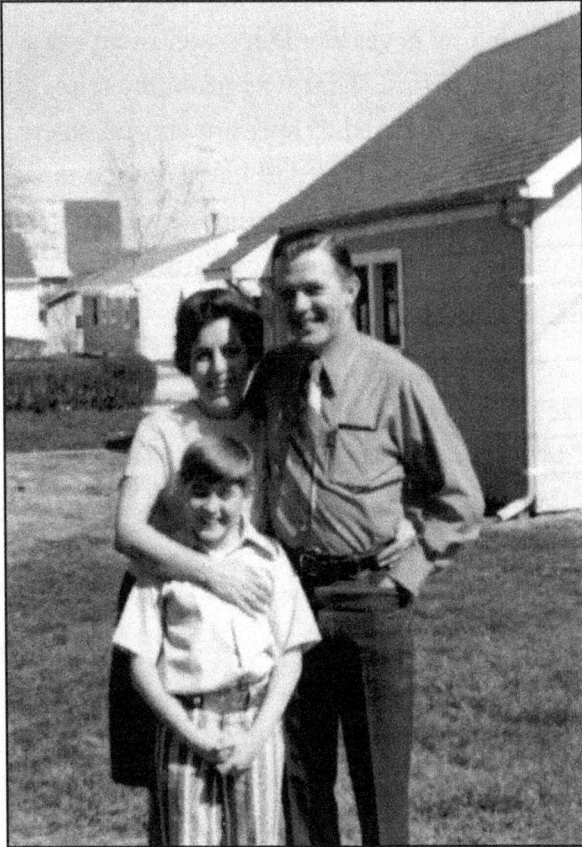

KEVIN AND HIS PARENTS IN 1973.

like most families with older and younger siblings, I'm sure I annoyed them. They probably thought our dad was too easy on me, letting me get away with things that he never would have let them get away with years before. That was probably true, but I wasn't around when they were growing up, so I really can't say. I suspect that dad had softened in some ways by the time I was born, but he was still pretty tough. He was a strict man by nature who lived by a standard of rules that we were expected to follow.

As I look back, I don't deny that he was a strict leader of our family, but I knew he loved me. I saw it in how he provided and in how he took an interest in me. I was able to see his work ethic and his discipline as a way of showing that he cared. We didn't use a lot of words, but I truly felt heard, understood, and loved by my dad.

When I was fourteen years old, my world was turned upside down when my dad died suddenly of a stroke. My siblings were older and had families of their own, leaving just me and my mom at home. I was lost without any sense of safety, comfort, or the predictability that I had once known.

My mom was so devastated by the loss of her rock and soulmate, that I was afraid talking about how the loss of my dad affected me would only make her pain worse. Walls began to go up between us, or maybe those walls were already there and I just didn't realize it until dad was no longer with us; I don't know for sure. I had lost my rock too. But I also felt like I had lost my voice.

I was fourteen at the time, which was probably the age dad was when he had to quit school. Questions run through my mind, wondering what he may have felt like. Did he ever feel unwanted by the father who raised him? Did he have feelings of not knowing who he was without knowing his biological dad? Did he ever wonder if he fully belonged in the family who raised him? When he quit school to work and take care of the family, did he feel like he had lost his voice too? I'll never know. I can only wonder if thoughts like this may have crossed his mind just like they were crossing mine. Even if I was misguided by these questions, they led me to a theme that I have carried my entire life: I am unwanted.

At that time, life was serious and the business of just getting through the day took its toll until, about six months after my dad passed away, I discovered a new "friend" that helped me find my voice—alcohol.

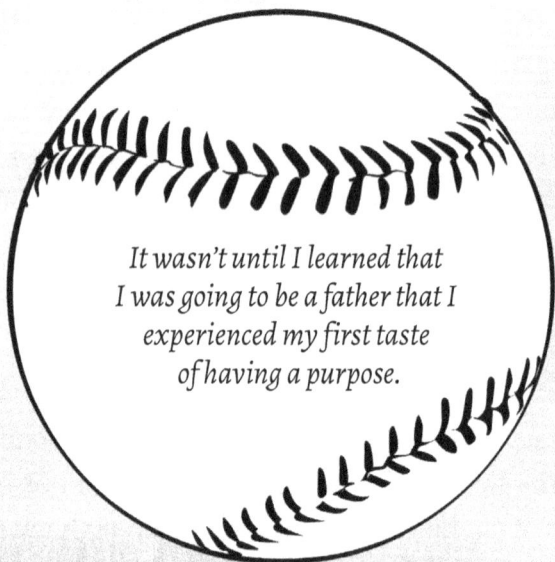

*It wasn't until I learned that
I was going to be a father that I
experienced my first taste
of having a purpose.*

Everyone else my age was drinking, so it didn't seem like a big deal. I suspect that all of our parents actually knew and expected that we drank. Drinking was controllable and seemed harmless. On the outside, it was a fun way to pass the time with my friends and I felt like I belonged. I had courage. I had a voice. On the inside, it helped me deal with the pain that I couldn't talk about.

After high school, I discovered that I actually preferred marijuana over alcohol and it was hangover-free. I had what I call a "healthy" relationship with pot usage. I smoked just enough to calm the nerves and numb the pain, but not miss work. I couldn't identify any problems with the drug and so it was easy to pretend that I was okay. Working, drinking, and smoking were a pretty normal way of life for me. It was familiar. It was how I lived and celebrated. It was how I hid. I was desperately seeking some kind of purpose in my life, but none of it, not even work, could fill that longing.

It wasn't until I learned that I was going to be a father that I experienced my first taste of having a purpose.

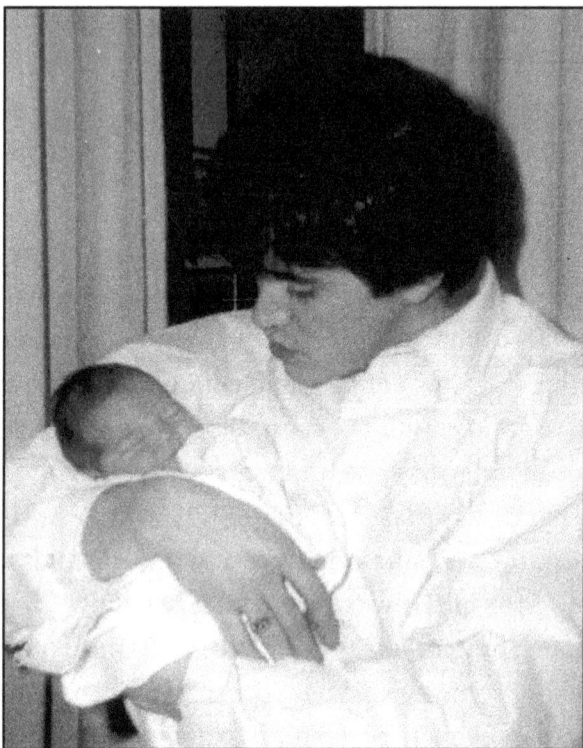

MY PURPOSE WAS BORN.

CHAPTER FOUR

Melissa

*"Furthermore, because we are united with
Christ, we have received an inheritance from
God, for he chose us in advance, and he makes
everything work out according to his plan."*

Ephesians 1:11 (NLT)

The foundation for my own marriage was built on Christ. I can't think of any better miracle than the fact that I have a healthy relationship with my husband in spite of what I learned and experienced growing up. I guess it's never too late for a miracle.

The relationship with my dad was a different story. I could see the changes in him, and he was persistently trying to pursue a relationship with me. I kind of went along with it all, holding him at arm's length and expecting the other shoe to fall.

As a little girl growing up, I don't have many clear memories of my dad other than he worked and would come home drunk or get drunk at home. He had his rules and expectations, but when he tried to correct my behavior, my mom would undermine him and tell me something different. She didn't seem to like him very much.

I remember a time when I was a teenager that dad came home drunk and he told me that he never would have married my mom if she hadn't gotten pregnant with me. I wasn't supposed to happen, and dad made it perfectly clear that he had done the *responsible thing* and married my mom. Couldn't we see that he had provided for his family for all these years? Was I was supposed to appreciate the fact that my dad had done the *right thing*? How was I supposed to respond? What I heard that day was that I wasn't wanted, and my parents had been going through life completely miserable with one another and their lives. It felt like it was all my fault.

When the words, "if it wasn't for you," whirled inside my mind, I contemplated suicide. My dad didn't seem to love me or care about what I had to say. He never asked me about my life and certainly never showed that he cared about how I felt. I can't

WHILE I WAS STILL SKEPTICAL OF HAVING
A RELATIONSHIP WITH MY DAD, THE SMILES HERE
ARE REAL; PROOF THAT DAD'S OBEDIENCE WAS
WORKING ON THE INSIDE.

_____❤_____

*When I began attending church
with my dad, I learned that I had a
Heavenly Father who cared for me.*

_____❤_____

recall a single time he told me he was proud of me or encouraged me. So maybe if I was gone, my parents could split apart. The pain would end for everyone—including me.

Later, when I began attending church with my dad, I learned that I had a Heavenly Father who cared for me. That was a miracle worth holding onto. I began to see some positive changes in my dad's life, but this whole father-daughter thing was fragile at best. I knew it wouldn't last. It would be less painful to move on without my dad in my life and, as a new military wife, moving wouldn't look like running away. Distance would make it difficult for him to maintain a relationship with me. Besides, he never cared about me all those years I was around. Why should I care now?

CHAPTER FIVE

Kevin

"For I know the plans I have for you,"
declares the LORD,
"plans to prosper you and not harm you,
plans to give you a hope and a future."

Jeremiah 29:11 (NIV)

My own father parented with rules, which I didn't
have any trouble following until after he died.
As a free-spirited person, my parents knew that I was
a boundary pusher and always challenged the rules.
Even so, my dad parented that way and I respected
the hard lines. I think that is why my relationship
with my dad worked. Then, he was gone.

My mom was not incredibly nurturing, but I knew
that she loved me. I had a harder time connecting
with her than I did with my dad. Looking back at the

period after my dad died, I wonder if she may have been afraid that she would lose me as well. My mom never remarried after dad's passing; she told me she didn't think she could get so lucky twice.

Even after the death of my dad, I never forgot how close my parents had been. My dad cherished my mom and I never heard him raise his voice to her or talk to her in any disrespectful way. In the short time I remember my parents together, I saw that they were united. They couldn't be pitted against one another. They were good people who truly loved each other well. It was the kind of relationship I hoped for.

When I first met my wife, we each came into the relationship with our own set of baggage. She was looking to escape from the environment of a controlling father. I wanted to be the one to rescue her. Maybe it's a guy thing, but I wanted to be the hero in her life.

My biggest piece of baggage was not feeling like I had a voice. Growing up, I didn't have a say in much, but was simply expected to act a certain way and follow the rules. Not doing so was unacceptable—period. There was no discussion about behavior or what might have happened to cause it. As a married man, when I had a strong thought or opinion, my wife interpreted that as being controlling. It's ironic that this same feeling is what I thought I was saving her from. Our partnership became passive-aggressive and I looked for intimacy in alcohol and marijuana. Stuffing my feelings, numbing my pain, and exploding in anger became a familiar pattern for expressing myself.

Our baggage and unhealthy habits are what we had in common and I don't know if we were truly *meant to be*. I hadn't been thinking marriage until I heard the words, "I'm pregnant." I wish I could say that this was the time that I had my "come to Jesus moment" and that my motives were loving and pure. Here's what I did know: I was going to be a father. I needed to do the right thing and follow the rules which were simple; I would marry the mother of my child and provide for my new and growing family. I did what my dad would have done.

I found great purpose in these tasks of planning, preparing, and providing. I had been searching for this for a long time and although I may have been misguided, I now had something I'd never had before—motivation.

When my daughter, Melissa, entered this world, I believe she saved my life. The bad habits slowed, and I filled my time with what I thought were good habits. All of the various jobs I worked, all of the

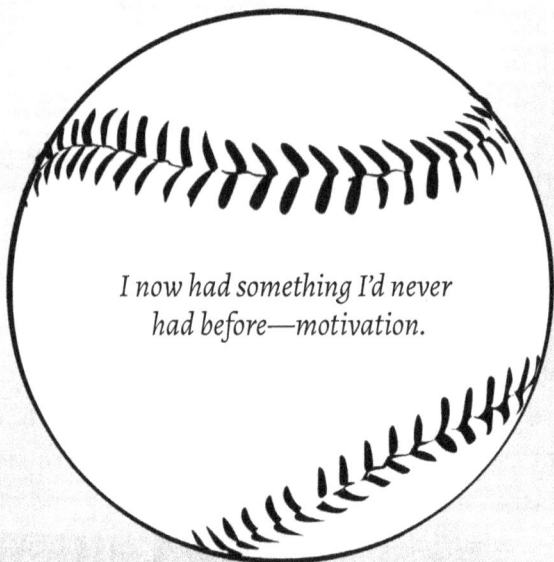

I now had something I'd never had before—motivation.

hours logged, the paychecks—it all had meaning. I was providing food, shelter and clothing for my family. Five years later we had a son, Bradley.

In those early years, I did the things that were expected of me and what I believed my dad would have done. Not only for the family he helped provide for while he was growing up, but for his wife and children too. Drinking with my buddies seemed like a socially acceptable way of spending down time and blowing off the steam that would build up after a work week. I was smoking pot here and there, but I was doing my job, fulfilling my responsibilities, and I didn't see anything wrong with any of it at the time.

My wife didn't share this perspective and she was very vocal about it. It became a source of conflict in our marriage for years and, over time, she became very unhappy with me. She didn't want me to talk about these issues because she would feel controlled. As a response, I would stuff my feelings and hide them in alcohol and marijuana. Instead of leaving me, she talked to others about my failures as a husband, father, and as a person. She may not have left me at this time, but she certainly didn't seem like she wanted me around.

My children grew up seeing a mom who didn't support their dad, and a dad who was always working, drinking, or using a controlled substance. A dad who didn't talk until all of the things he stuffed down exploded in anger. They saw parents who didn't work together to solve problems and a marital relationship that revolved around negativity. My wife was constantly unhappy with me and we started living separate lives, parallel to one another.

I finally decided that I didn't care anymore. Although I continued to follow in my own dad's footsteps and fulfill my responsibilities as a father by working and providing for my family, I didn't feel wanted and decided there was no use trying to pretend that I was. I had hoped having a family was my newfound purpose and would change how I felt on the inside. But the faces of my children and the voice of my wife only magnified my feelings of being unwanted.

I know the birth of my daughter saved me from a path of complete destruction. It would take many years and bumps in the road before I saw my children as the miracle that they were: a gift from God. He was asking me to pick up my brokenness and offer it to Him so that He could put it back together. I wasn't sure what that would look like, but I couldn't give up on my relationships with my wife and kids.

After all, my Heavenly Father had never given up on me.

CHAPTER SIX

Melissa

*"God blesses those who work for peace, for they
will be called the children of God."*

Matthew 5:9 (NLT)

After Robert and I married, I continued to live near my family while he was off to basic training. It seemed inevitable that we would not be sticking around the area, and I planned to move where he was stationed. God had another plan, though, and Robert ended up being sent to Korea for a year unaccompanied, while I remained closer to home for longer than I had counted on. God obviously knew that dad and I needed more time together.

At that time, my brother was in his early years of high school, and from my perspective, he was getting

Melissa,

Many times I think of you.
I just wanted to tell you
I always wish for all good
things to come your way. We
have said many things towards
one another, It could be easy
to say who cares. I am proud
of you and you have many gifts
to offer people. Always set your
sights high. Whatever you focus
on grows. Here is another
Quote I came across recently
that made sense to me. I
Hope you get something from it
to.
"Refuse to make excuses or blame
anyone for anything"

THIS IS A NOTE DAD SENT TO ME. AT THE TIME
I RECEIVED IT, I WAS STILL SKEPTICAL OF THERE
BEING HOPE FOR OUR RELATIONSHIP.

nothing but love, support, and encouragement from my dad. What did I get when I was that age? On a good day, ignored. Watching their relationship caused bitterness, jealousy, and anger to build up inside of me. I kept trying to tell myself that it really didn't matter.

I was happy that dad had found Christ and he really did seem to be genuine. It wasn't like dad went around shouting from the rooftops about how Jesus changed his life. He was too humble for that. Maybe he was too scared and afraid that no one close to him would care? Or, like I was thinking, maybe he knew that sooner or later he would trip up and the changes wouldn't stick. I decided to keep my distance. I didn't care to rock any boats or dredge up hurts from the past. Our relationship was fragile, to say the least. We still argued, and if anyone told me that I was even a little bit like my dad, it drove me endlessly crazy. I simply wanted to move on, build my own relationship with Christ alongside my husband—apart from my dad.

Physical separation from my family and my dad felt like a fresh start, but apparently dad had no intention of letting the geographical distance stop him from being a pain in my butt. I tried to run away from having anything more than a *maybe-I'll-see-you-at-Christmas* relationship. The further I ran, however, the more dad continued to pursue a relationship with me. He said that he wasn't trying to be pushy, but God had other plans and he was simply trying to be obedient. When I heard that, I felt the Holy Spirit nudge my conscience, whispering to me that if I was going to be obedient to my Heavenly Father, then I needed to listen and believe that there was something more going on with my earthly father.

♥

*If I was going to be obedient to
my Heavenly Father, then I needed
to listen and believe that there
was something more going on
with my earthly father.*

♥

CHAPTER SEVEN

Kevin

"And I am certain that God,
who began the good work within you,
will continue his work until it is finally finished
on the day when Christ Jesus returns."

Philippians 1:6 (NLT)

Through all of the years of searching, I was
running away from Jesus. Thankfully, He never
stopped pursuing me and was determined to get
my attention. One of those times happened in
September of 1995. I was away from home for work.
After a sales meeting, we headed out for drinks as
usual. Some of us needed to drive quite a distance
home and, although many of them left after a few
drinks, I decided to keep drinking with the local
guys.

On my way home, I picked up a six-pack for the drive. Halfway home, I realized that I was starving and stopped by Hardees, devouring two sandwiches in five minutes. I have no recollection of the fifteen miles that I drove on the interstate after that stop, but when I opened my eyes, I was about to hit the back of a semitrailer. I jerked the wheel just in time, but lost control of the car, bouncing off the trailer, and I ended up in the ditch.

I should have died in that accident. It is only by the grace of God that I am still here. I didn't know God then. I didn't have a relationship with Him. I knew of Him and believed He existed, but that was it. But in my heart, I knew that there was no logical reason I was still alive. I even talked to people about *God's grace*, but I really didn't understand what that meant. If I had died that night, it would not have been good.

Though I didn't understand it then, keeping me alive until I did know Him and accept Him into my life was the gracious miracle of that accident. I was arrested for a DUI that night, which slowed me down on my path towards destruction, but I still continued to run from God for another seven years before He grabbed ahold of my heart. Even as I gained speed,

God continued to throw in speed bumps to slow me down.

One of those bumps was an outburst with my boss. I had had enough and was going to quit. Some of my co-workers, however, genuinely cared about my well-being. They saw someone who was hurting, and they were willing to journey along a healing path with me. This was a wake-up call. My co-workers had no reason to become involved. People caring about me without expectations or ulterior motives felt foreign. Instead of being unemployed, I was reassigned to a different department and, after a work evaluation, was recommended for counseling.

For about a year, I behaved, walked the straight and narrow, and did all the right things. I even earned a one-year chip from AA. On the outside, things appeared to be looking up, but the inside still had some trouble that needed to be addressed. I wasn't willing or didn't know how to manage my loneliness, worthlessness, and anger. I didn't feel loved and I was dying. The outward motions did not match the inner feelings. I lost friendships with people who truly cared, even as I recognized that God had put them in my life, and He orchestrated good through them.

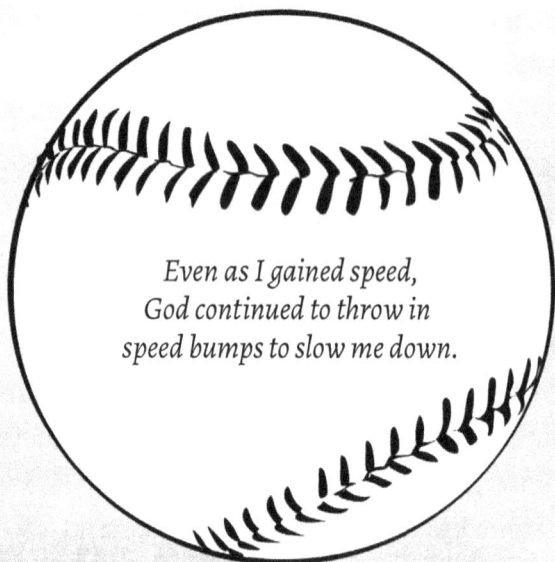

Even as I gained speed,
God continued to throw in
speed bumps to slow me down.

I once heard a pastor say, "The only good in me is the Jesus in me." I didn't have Jesus then and I ended up losing the job. If I was God, I would have given up on me and let Kevin die in that accident or continue down the path of destruction. I had caused so much damage to myself and in my relationships with others.

God placed some incredible people in my life during some of my most destructive times. At about my lowest point, a guy named Mike gave me a job framing houses. I didn't have a license, so Mike picked me up each day for work. Seeing him care enough to go out of his way kept me out of those rock-bottom places. Although the job was a positive experience for me, we did some drinking after work. But he was a good man. You don't throw the baby out with the bathwater, right? I found great purpose in having work and a paycheck. There is nothing worse for a man than not having a job or purpose.

I finally surrendered my heart to Christ when I was 40 years old. My wife wasn't convinced of the changes that I was in the process of making. Although my daughter came to know Christ, she still did not want much to do with her old man. But I didn't want to give up. When Melissa moved away, I kept trying to pursue a relationship with her and prove to her that I wasn't going to give up on us. I knew that God could heal the damage I had caused. She had every right to walk away, and she wasn't making anything easy. I hadn't made it easy on God either and, just like He refused to give up on me, I refused to give up on her.

CHAPTER EIGHT

Melissa

"Make allowance for each other's faults, and
forgive anyone who offends you. Remember, the
Lord forgave you, so you must forgive others."

Colossians 3:13 (NLT)

I moved away fully expecting to have no relationship with my father. But when my dad wants something, he goes after it. He never gives up. Up until this point, I had only seen this play out negatively. I was beginning, however, to see a shift.

After Robert completed basic training and served for a year in Korea, we moved to Fort Bliss, Texas. Not long after, dad started going on mission trips that were just across the border from our new home. Once, he asked if he could visit us before his mission team left. It wasn't as bad as I thought because I was able to help dad's group make preparations to leave. Helping him with specific tasks took the pressure off trying to pretend or work at some kind of relationship.

He stayed again for a few days on the return trip but seemed distant—cold even. Dad was shutting down, was very quiet, and withdrawn. I interpreted his behavior as shutting me out. It was a trigger for me, I would feel unwanted, and I would get upset. But I began to realize that after a trip, when he decompressed and tried to process all that he had witnessed and experienced, it wasn't the same withdrawing that I remembered from growing up. When he was able to open up, I learned that his heart had been broken for the people he had met and worked with. His quietness did not mean that he was trying to distance himself, but that he was pondering the depravity he had seen. He was journeying through how amazing God is and the ways He would always show up on these mission trips. Since that first trip, he has gone on more short-term missions than I can count. Each one changed and broke him in different and beautiful ways.

It was probably after his first trip when I realized that his faith wasn't just a phase. Even though he had

You really are a precious
gift from above. When I think
of what God has done in our
relationship and especially in
my heart I am overwhelmed.
I pray that in the depth of
your soul you learn to _celebrate_
your _birthday_ with a God
perspective. He is radically
crazy about you.

Happy Birthday

Love Dad

Jer. 1:5

A BIRTHDAY CARD; ONE OF THE
MANY CARDS I SAVED FROM MY DAD.

a hard time expressing what he was thinking and feeling, my eyes and my heart began to open a little bit more. I wasn't just seeing the changes, I felt them. Dad has never been the same since he began serving God on these trips.

♥

*I wasn't just seeing the changes,
I felt them.*

♥

CHAPTER NINE

Kevin

"Though he may stumble, he will not fall,
for the LORD upholds him with his hand."

Psalms 37:24 (NIV)

In the early years of handing the pieces of my life to Jesus, the devil would constantly remind me of my failures. He'd get into my head and try to make me believe that I couldn't fix all the hurt and pain I had caused to my family. He would tell me that I wasn't good enough. He would try and twist the truth of God's word into a lie. He planted the fear in my heart that I was destined to stay right where I was, that things were too far gone, and that I'd never move forward in any area of my life, especially in my relationships with my wife and children.

Working on my relationship with my son was easier than with Melissa. He was a teenager living at home. I was able to help him plug in to a youth group and I volunteered to be a part of it. My son was able to see the changes I was making in my life daily, and that Jesus was the reason for those changes. We weren't constantly talking about the Bible, faith, Jesus, church, and religion. I felt like no one wanted to hear my words, so I used my actions and reactions to point to Jesus. This didn't always play out in a perfect way.

The difference between the Kevin-before-Jesus and the Kevin-after-Jesus wasn't that I never got angry again, said the wrong thing, or messed up, because I still screwed up quite a bit. When I did, though, the Kevin-after-Jesus was quick to admit his faults and apologize, unlike the Kevin-before-Jesus, who was quick to become angry, place blame, and turn to alcohol for comfort.

Melissa didn't see this side of me. Building a relationship with her wasn't easy since she had moved on with her life, was married, and lived hours away. I didn't know how to do it. No matter how many miles separated us, both physically and emotionally, I knew that our relationship was one of the biggest broken pieces of my life. God wanted me to hand it over to him, even if I kept dropping it and picking it back up over and over again.

I had always been hard on Melissa when she was growing up. All she received from me were rules. A relationship with me was a foreign concept. Admittedly, even as I was discouraged with the slow progress in our relationship, I couldn't blame her. Since she wasn't around, my actions could not be a witness to the changes Christ was making in my life. I was going to have to use words.

I started sending Melissa text messages with notes from devotionals that I was reading. I wasn't trying to preach to her, I just wanted her to know that she was in my thoughts and that I was praying for her. One year on her birthday, I wanted to send something special, showing that I loved her and that I was proud of who she had grown up to become. I was honored to be her dad, but she didn't know it. I knew my words would fall on deaf ears. She didn't want to hear from me. Even if she did, I was certain she would be skeptical. Everything I wanted to say was true, but she wouldn't believe it coming from me.

Feeling stuck about what to say, I turned to my devotional and read, "Before I formed you in the

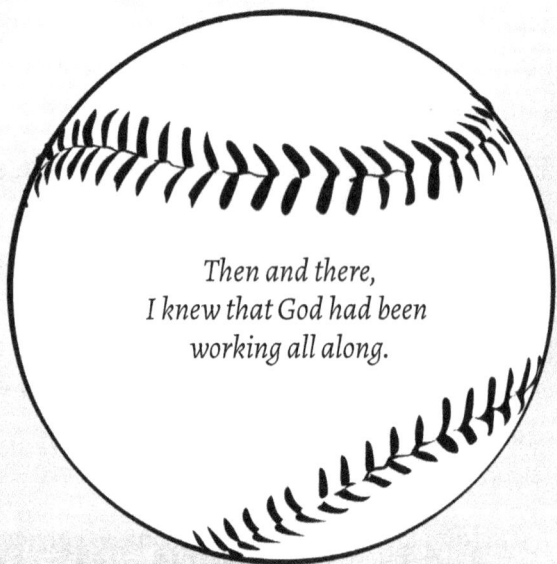

Then and there,
I knew that God had been
working all along.

womb, I knew you, before you were born, I set you apart" (Jeremiah 1:5). I hit my knees. The conviction ran deep. This little girl of mine was a gift from God. He is the One who knit her together. She is special and loved because she was created by God, not because of anything I did or didn't do.

I sent a snapshot of that devotional to her and wrote all of the things I wanted to say. I wished her a happy birthday, but I also told her that I loved her and was proud of her. I apologized for not being the dad she needed when she was growing up and for not treating her as the treasure and gift that she truly was. To this day, I continue to send her encouraging notes and remind her that I'm praying for her.

Many years have passed since that first birthday text, and I'm sure Melissa was less than excited to receive it. She didn't care. She was mad and hurt. But I continued to send passages from the Bible or inspirational quotes and cards that I thought she might like. I wanted her to know that she was always on my mind, that I wanted to connect with her, and that I loved her, even if she didn't love me. Sometimes I would send her a note when memories of things I had done wrong would surface. Quite often, these thoughts would sneak up on me, along with their accompanying lies from the devil.

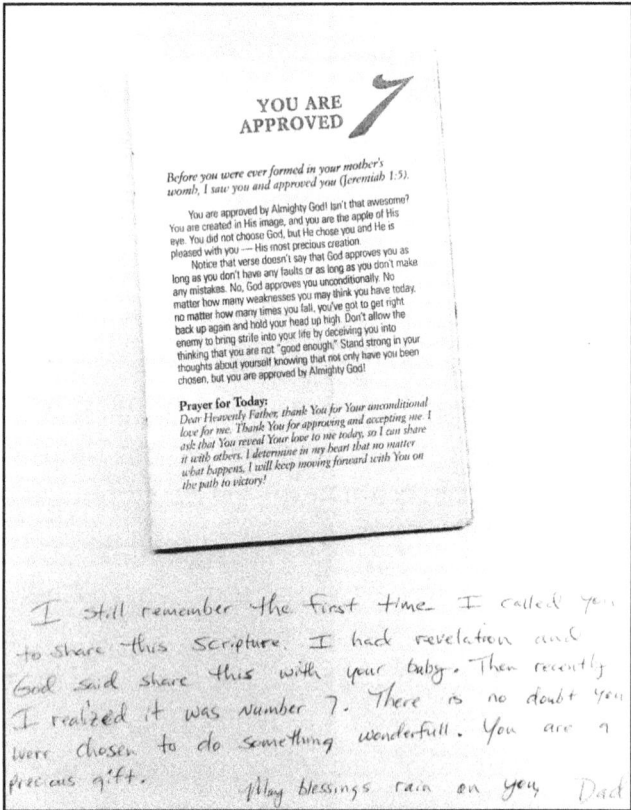

A TEXT MESSAGE THAT I SENT MY LITTLE GIRL,
WHO SENT IT BACK TO ME, YEARS LATER,
AT JUST THE RIGHT TIME—IT MAY AS WELL
HAVE BEEN A TEXT FROM GOD.

When this happened, I learned to look to scripture and pray. I'd send Melissa a note with the words God had given me as a way of combating the bad memories that would surface.

One day, years later, I was feeling pretty down and unsure of my purpose and direction. I often allowed myself to sit for a while in my depression. At this very moment of hopelessness, my phone pinged.

It was a text from Melissa.

She had sent me one of the notes that I had sent to her years before. As it turned out, she had saved every one of the prayers, devotional snapshots, and notes of encouragement that I had sent her. On that day, without knowing my state of mind or how I was feeling, she sent the exact words I needed in order to lift my spirit. She had used my very own method of combatting bad memories and sent it right back to me.

Then and there, I knew that God had been working all along. Before I came to accept Him as my Savior, He pursued me and never gave up on me. He used every circumstance in my life to point to Himself, whether or not I realized it at the time. He wanted a relationship with me even when I kept running the opposite direction. Melissa didn't know that

I needed those words and I didn't know she had been saving the text messages all along, but God did. I began to see just what God can do when we obediently hand these things over to Him. He is so amazing in how He works.

CHAPTER TEN

Melissa

*"Above all, clothe yourselves with love, which
binds us all together in perfect harmony."*

Colossians 3:14 (NLT)

♥

Dad used to send me these annoying text messages
and cards. Okay, the messages weren't necessarily annoying; they were actually kind of helpful. The
fact that they came from him, however, annoyed me.

When he first started sending me texts, I would
think *Yeah, whatever. Who was this guy? Did he really
think that the hurt would just magically melt away because
he sent me a Bible verse or devotional?* It's not as simple
as that.

Even so, a part of me would be touched by the
message. I found myself saving them and reading

DEAR Melissa   JUNE 15 2009

    ON THIS FATHER'S DAY I WANT
to say I am sorry. I know there
ARE MANY hurts AND DISApPOINTMENTS
that NEED healing. I take full responsibility
and pray that you will forgive me.
I can remember when you were born
and how small and prescious you were.
I was unprepared for all that would
come. My heart was to provide a
great life for you and your mom.
I worked very hard at the providing
part but failed at the emotional
side. So today if I could say
anything I would tell you, to
remember always No matter what there
is a God who saw you before time
began, He has a great plan for you
and He loves you with a love I
can not understand but I am committed
to learn it until the day I go home
to Jesus. THE trials in our life are
to build our character. You are a
fathers blessing and if you will help
me I will work on being the father
of your dreams.

Love
DAD

DAD SENT ME A LETTER ON FATHER'S DAY

them every once in a while. As he persisted without any reciprocation from me, my heart started to soften. I came to realize that he wasn't trying to pretend that everything was okay behind an inspiring message. In almost every note, he apologized. His thoughts gave me a glimpse into what he was thinking or going through during his own years of parenting. Now, as an adult, I could see that he had gone through what most people go through—trying to find purpose and meaning while stumbling along the way. Isn't that everyone? Why should my dad be any different? Why was I holding on to an unrealistic expectation of him?

With miles of separation, my dad replaced unplanned visits with cards and letters that spanned over several years. I saved them all. As I opened each letter, I got to know my dad and learned a little more about where he came from. Even some of his mistakes started to make sense. As an adult, I grew to see that he had done the best that he could have with what he had to work with. I even started asking myself if I could blame him.

In his letters, he took full responsibility for each of his actions, blaming no one but himself. He was adamant in his willingness to do anything to turn

———————— ♥ ————————

*With miles of separation,
my dad replaced unplanned visits
with cards and letters that spanned
over several years.*

———————— ♥ ————————

things around while recognizing that our history was dysfunctional at best. I could see that the man I had spent my entire life hating, and who I thought hated me, believed that I was one of the greatest blessings of his life.

The more I learned about my dad, the more I realized that I did love him. I began to understand that his lack of a father contributed to his focus on responsibility rather than on relationships. I also suspect that from the earliest stages of parenting, my mom and dad didn't agree on their roles. When Mom would trump dad after he tried to correct me, my interpretation was that dad was always wrong. Looking back, I have begun to heal from my misunderstanding that dad didn't want me or love me. On most days, I think he was trying his best.

Through letters, I began to believe that dad wanted the best for me, even if I chose not to let him into my life. He wrote that he was in my corner no matter what, and I realized that I wanted him there.

I always had.

CHAPTER ELEVEN

Kevin

"The Lord is not slow in keeping his
promise, as some understand slowness.
Instead he is patient with you,
not wanting anyone to perish,
but everyone to come to repentance."

2 Peter 3:9 (NIV)

My relationship with Melissa certainly seemed to be heading in the right direction. It hadn't been quick, and it took literal years for us to get below the surface. As we were getting to know each other, Melissa seemed to genuinely care and ask about me and how I grew up. She began asking me for my opinion. At the same time, she would share the hurt that she carried. Hurt that had come directly from me. My destructive patterns as a father, a husband,

and a person had cut deep. I felt extreme remorse for all the pain that I had caused. I wished I could go back to comfort the little girl who had to deal with so much negativity from her parents. Since time only moves in one direction, I did my best to apologize every chance I could and comfort the young woman in front of me.

I wish I could say that my destructive patterns completely dissolved during this time. We still had arguments during this journey and they usually stemmed from feelings that I wasn't being respected. In the past, when I wasn't respected by my wife or my children, that would trigger anger. The disrespect I felt during this time of rebuilding our relationship, however, was most likely a misunderstanding. Based on how I treated Melissa while she was growing up, she had no reason to show me any kind of respect. My actions were not her fault and I struggled against constantly beating myself up over that. Even as we were both trying, my greatest fear was that I would mess up again and Melissa would choose to completely give up on me.

My patterns were changing. When we had an argument, I would apologize and take ownership for my actions. I stopped making excuses and saying

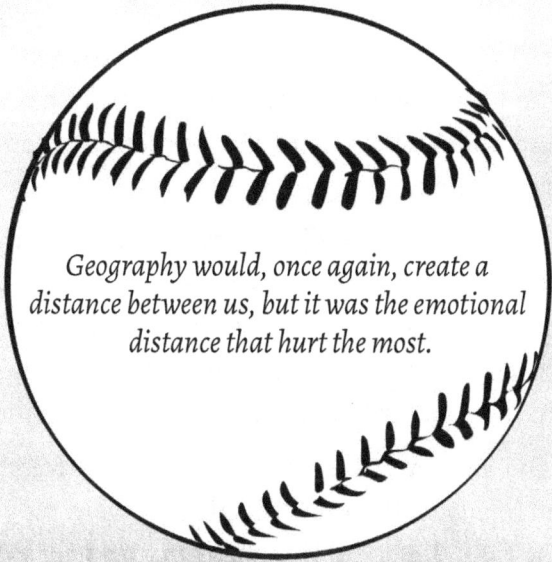

Geography would, once again, create a distance between us, but it was the emotional distance that hurt the most.

things like, "Well you did this so that's why I did that." Instead of always wanting her to understand where I was coming from, I wanted to let her talk and to understand where she was coming from. It was humbling.

I didn't have a stellar track record for authentic apologies, so they weren't always well received. Historically, they looked more like pointing fingers and placing blame. Although I was gradually changing, Melissa probably had a hard time believing me.

Our journey was the proverbial "one step forward, two steps back," but essentially, we were moving in the right direction. If we had an argument when I visited with her, I would usually try and patch things up before I left, wanting to make things right. Geography would, once again, create a distance between us, but it was the emotional distance that hurt the most.

Each time I made the choice to not give up trying, I was reminded of how Jesus continued to pursue me. I could have grabbed on to Him many times before I truly heard the message of salvation. Time and time again, Jesus tried to get my attention, but it took me forty years to finally receive His message and the gift of salvation. I determined that no matter how badly I had screwed up or how long it took to heal the relationship with my daughter, I was not giving up either.

Although I could never pinpoint a specific moment or think of what I had done differently, things definitely began to improve somewhere along the way.

CHAPTER TWELVE

Melissa

"Get rid of all bitterness, rage, anger, harsh words, and slander, as well as all types of evil behavior. Instead, be kind to each other, tenderhearted, forgiving one another, just as God through Christ has forgiven you."

Ephesians 4:31-32 (NLT)

❤

I don't have many clear memories of my childhood, but I do remember that our home was full of tension, bitterness, and anger. Dad just wasn't around much and, if he was, there was a good chance that he was angry or drunk. Probably both. My mom rarely had anything nice to say about him and that certainly influenced my opinion of dad. Somehow, throughout this story, I continued to believe that there was supposed to be more—that it was supposed to be better. But because I had such

Dear Melissa,

Feb 7, 2004

It seems hard to believe you are 21 years old today. As I reflect back to the beginning I was just a kid when we had you. I was unprepared, scared and not sure what to do. But some inner strength inside of me at the time moved me forward. I realize today it was God working in my life. Many times in life you come to crossroads I pray you will always make decisions out of love because it is the only path to happiness. There is a lot of history between us,

but today on your 21st birthday I wanted you to know once again I am proud of the person you are inside. Beware of anger, fear, hate, jealousy, envy and all other destructive emotions. They will lead you down a dark path. Every day is an opportunity to make a difference in someones life. Life is a precious gift don't waste it. The past is a gift learn from it and use the knowledge to make a better today. So on this day, your 21st birthday I pray it is one to remember. God loves you and you are special.

"A failure can not over take me if My desire to succeed is strong enough."

love Dad
(617-27329)

MY 21ST BIRTHDAY CARD FROM DAD

a hard time letting go of old patterns, I was afraid to hope that our relationship could be more than it was—that it could be better.

There was a ten-year time span when God was clearly working on both of our hearts. I was learning some of the reasons why weaknesses defined my family, and anger and addiction defined my dad. These were the issues that surrounded my childhood. It makes me sad, now, to see how good intentions of hard work and providing for a family were twisted by evil. It's not a lie or small thing that the Bible says the devil is out there, prowling around like a roaring lion seeking to destroy and devour. Evil came close to beating my dad and nearly won out in our relationship, even after we both accepted Christ. My dad continues to say that just as Jesus didn't give up pursuing him, he wasn't going to give up pursuing a relationship with me.

The more I got to know my dad, the more I wanted to know. That is not to say that we didn't have arguments. We certainly did. Old patterns die hard and I learned that this was true for both of us. Only now, during these times, I couldn't just pin the blame all on dad. Instead of always pointing at him, I began to self-evaluate, learning my own triggers and how to navigate my feelings. I had learned that God commanded me to love and respect my dad no matter what.

During one of his visits when my husband and I lived in Washington State, we had one last, big blow-up. I honestly don't remember what our fight was about, I just remember that my dad genuinely wanted to talk things out. He didn't want to bury anything or ignore the feelings that were taking place. It was on this visit, after this fight, I realized something pretty significant . . . I was the one holding back.

Most likely, my dad had always wanted to talk things out after an argument. I hate dragging things out too, but I wasn't truly accepting his apologies before. Maybe I wasn't cooled down enough or maybe I felt like my dad didn't apologize the way I thought he should. After that last blow-up, God showed me that I had ownership in our fallouts, and the forgiveness that God gave to me was the forgiveness that I needed to give to my dad. Once I understood that, our ten-year journey to healing took a major turn towards honest restoration.

The difference that I see in my dad and in the things he continues to do, is truly a remarkable and inspiring story of transformation and

*Every day I see my father
becoming more like a reflection of
his Heavenly Father.*

obedience to God. People have always told me that my father and I are a lot alike. That comment used to feel like daggers. Now it makes me proud to hear that I am just like my dad. How could I want to be anything less than him? He is strong, obedient, loving, and has the heart of a servant. He doesn't claim to be perfect and he tries everyday. These all feel like great traits to aspire to. Every day I see my father becoming more like a reflection of his Heavenly Father.

The more I learn about my dad, the more I love him. He has continued to pick up the broken pieces of his story and hand them over to God. Some of these stories are still being written. Some of them aren't turning out the way that I know my dad has hoped. Our relationship, however, has been redeemed.

Kevin

"Jesus looked at them and said,
'With man this is impossible, but
not with God; all things are
possible with God.' '

Mark 10:27 (NIV)

✕

There is a new lightness about me that began on the day I gave my heart to Jesus. In that moment, all the things I carried with me and the areas of life I tried to control fell to the floor. Picking up each piece of my shattered life and handing it over to my Heavenly Father continues to be an exercise of strength and faith. There were some pretty heavy pieces. To be completely honest, there still are.

It's been eighteen years since my walk with Christ first began. Giving God control over every area of my life started with my relationship with

Melissa. It took ten years to see a miracle; thankfully, we both kept the course and experienced restoration. It could have been easy for either one of us to give up. In His mercy, God didn't allow that to happen.

I've also seen God bring redemption and a healthy perspective in other areas of my life. I give him my brokenness and watch Him put the pieces back together in a way that brings glory to Himself.

A lot of things about my story are uncomfortable to talk about. I'm not proud of my past. I'm not necessarily proud of every moment of my present. To be honest, there is a lot of shame involved in sharing some of the secrets that I've kept to myself. But over the years, I've learned that it's okay to be real and authentic, even when I am in the middle of a messy story.

I also learned that waiting on God is always worth it, even when it means letting go of something I held onto for a long time. My story with Melissa is proof of that. Not to say that every area of my life has ended with a miracle like the one I experienced with my daughter. Many of my prayers have not been answered the way I hoped. My first marriage unfortunately ended in a divorce. But I still share my story because I rest in the knowledge that God is in control. He holds the pen.

Waiting on God is
always worth it.

I also share my story because it releases the devil's hold on me. Even if I haven't seen healing and restoration in every area of my life, I have experienced the freedom promised when I am truthful. I've learned that fear—of what others think, of judgement, and in general—is a huge waste of time.

God is in the business of restoring stories. From the very first pages of the Bible to the current page in my own life, His purposes are always for my good and His glory. Will He redeem everything the way I want Him to? No. Do I trust that His plan is the best? I have to. God is good. Even when I struggle to see the good around me, I believe that He never changes. I pray that God will eventually show me the beauty in the brokenness, even if it's not on this side of heaven.

I still struggle with giving God control and then taking it back again. I'm a fixer—I want to hurry in and make things better for people when I see them sad or upset. I understand that God wired me to be this way, but I still have to constantly remind myself to follow His lead and that the outcome remains in His hands. It took me a long time to understand this. Living in the past, where I experienced shame and regret, does not do anything to help my present or future. It's okay to have a bad day, or even a bad

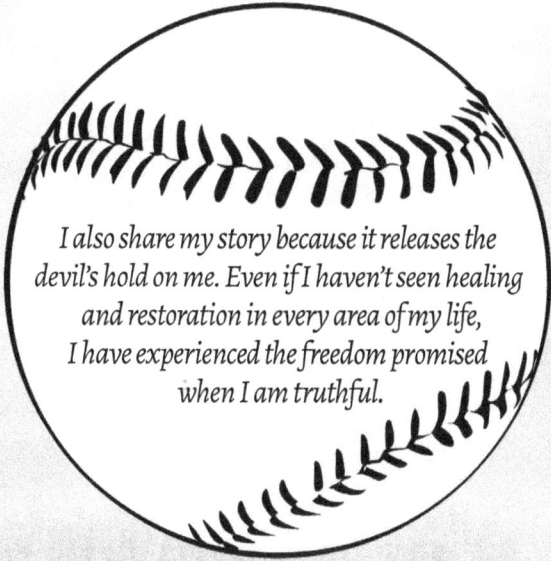

I also share my story because it releases the devil's hold on me. Even if I haven't seen healing and restoration in every area of my life, I have experienced the freedom promised when I am truthful.

God is in the business of restoring stories.

season. Everyone does. But I won't allow myself to pitch my tent and stay there.

I've found a sense of purpose and identity through this constant process of handing over my life to Christ. I've been a part of meaningful work on mission trips and through an organization called One Eighty. I've even found meaning in my job. I continue to make strides in my relationship with my son and his family. All of these things are good, but God has shown me that if I try and find my identity in anything other than Him, even the good things can become idols. My purpose in life, and all the pieces and parts of it, is to point to Christ. It's a good reminder that I'm really just a character in God's story. My character may not have started out on solid ground, but I want to finish strong.

The words on these pages are mostly about how God pursued me and how, through Him, my relationship with my daughter was restored. Putting the words on the page has also been a healing journey. In recording the story, I began to understand that this book has also been about forgiveness, dealing with the past, and generational family issues. It's about learning how to dream again and re-build things that were once broken. It's been a reminder that no matter how much time has gone by, God is never late. He is always right on time.

I've learned to never give up.

I chose the title of this book for two reasons. The first is that Christ never gave up on me, and through that, He showed me the importance of not giving up on my daughter, or any of the other broken pieces of my life and relationships.

My dad always used to say to me "Where there's a will, there's a way." I've come to the understanding that the real nugget of truth here is that when it's God's will, He will provide the way. No amount of strength or "will" on my part can change that.

The second reason I chose this title is because it isn't the entire truth when it comes to my story. The entire journey has really been about the one thing that I did have to give up: control.

Jesus was the ultimate example of this. Not only did He never give up on me, but He surrendered His own life for mine when He bore my sins on the cross.

Giving God control over every area of life doesn't always come naturally to me. But I'm learning that surrendering my will to God's will brings me to a place of peace. When my thoughts don't line up with His, I experience conflict. I want to be filled with peace.

God is always right on time.

My story isn't over, and neither is yours. You may feel like life is hopeless or that it is just not turning out the way you hoped it would. Maybe you are struggling with anger, addiction, purpose, relationships . . . your list, like my own, can go on and on. I'm right there with you, friend. I wrote this story as a testimony to God's faithfulness. But I also hope it encourages you in your faith.

Sometimes we need someone to walk alongside of us and to show genuine care with no other motive than that they do care. I experienced that with the men who I worked with and who were praying for me. I'd like to let you know that if you are reading this book, I have prayed for you as well.

If my story has impacted you in any way, I'd love to hear from you. Send a note to barkmank@gmail.com. Better yet, let's talk. Give me a call or text me at (309) 314-3549. I'll be here.

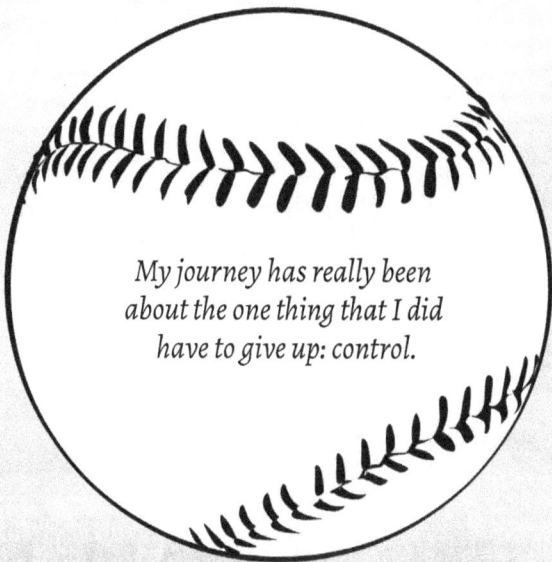

My journey has really been about the one thing that I did have to give up: control.

Melissa

"From the fullness of his grace we have all
received one blessing after another."

John 1:16 (NIV)

❤

Growing up, I didn't know what it was like really to have a Dad.

Today, I can't imagine living this beautiful, sometimes crazy life without him.

Growing up, I didn't understand or see everything going on behind the scenes.

Today, I can't imagine not knowing the stories of the people I love.

Growing up, I didn't witness love.

Today, I can't imagine not trying to be love and a witness every day.

This smile has been brought to you...

A CARD THAT I SENT TO MY DAD.
WE HAVE COME A LONG WAY.

To
Daddy

...by someone who believes in you!

Just wanted to drop you a few lines
and let you know I was thinking about.
Just know that no matter how far
BJ and I go, you will always be very
special to me... you're my daddy.
I love you so much! Thank you
for being such an incredible
mentor to me and BJ.

Love
Your Little Girl

The journey that God had for my dad and me was long and often felt impossible or like a complete waste of time. My dad's determination, through God's command, is no doubt what kept me from giving up, and a key reason that our relationship looks better today. My dad has become one of the greatest rocks in my life. He's my cheerleader. He's my counsel. He's my best friend. I look up to him. I rely on him. I pray he truly knows just how amazing and inspiring he really is, and that he is unconditionally loved by both his Creator and his daughter. We don't have to agree on every single thing the other says or does . . . that's what grace is for. Grace is what comes when you truly care about someone and don't want to let judgment drive a wedge between you.

To know my Father in Heaven is to love Him. To know dad, is to love him. What an inspiring parallel. Getting to know God and understanding the woman He wants me to be, led me to my dad. Grateful and blessed does not seem to fully describe my feelings enough, yet it's all I have.

If you're reading this and have a relationship(s) that needs restoration . . . please know that I believe in you and am praying for you! You are special. You are worth it. You can be redeemed.

God can heal your brokenness.

♥

To know my Father in Heaven is to love Him. To know dad, is to love him. What an inspiring parallel.

♥

Questions for Reflection and Discussion

———————❤———————

Kevin and Melissa's story include feelings that range from hopeless to healing. While you may not find yourself with the same father-daughter dynamics that the authors did, most people can relate to the temptation to give up when the mountain you're climbing is too steep. Use the questions, verses, and thoughts to write yourself into the story, *Never Give Up*.

1. Before accepting Christ, Kevin looked for purpose and satisfaction in work and financial security. Identity and purpose are common struggles for most people. Where do you find purpose? Is it for God's glory or your own?

_____

_____

_____

_____

_____

_____

_____

_____

_____

_____

_____

_____

_____

_____

_____

_____

2. Have you ever had anyone tell you they are praying for you? How did it make you feel? Is there someone you can offer to pray for today?

_____

_____

_____

_____

_____

_____

_____

_____

_____

_____

_____

_____

_____

_____

_____

_____

_____

_____

3. Proverbs 3:5 says "Trust in the Lord with all your heart and lean not on your own understanding," (NIV). What does this verse mean to you? What circumstances do you feel led to give over to God?

_____

_____

_____

_____

_____

_____

_____

_____

_____

_____

_____

_____

_____

_____

_____

_____

_____

4. Matthew 5:9 says that "God blesses those who work for peace, for they will be called children of God" (NLT). Are there any relationships in your life you feel called to pursue and mend?

_____

_____

_____

_____

_____

_____

_____

_____

_____

_____

_____

_____

_____

_____

_____

_____

_____

5. Melissa's knowledge of church and religion while growing up revolved around traditions within the church on the "big days." What is your church background? Did you grow up not understanding the meaning behind the words and actions at your church? Was the idea of having a relationship with Jesus ever modeled for you?

_____

_____

_____

_____

_____

_____

_____

_____

_____

_____

_____

_____

_____

_____

_____

6. "Make allowance for each other's faults and forgive anyone who offends you. Remember, the Lord forgave you, so you must forgive others" (Col 3:13 NLT). What situations in your life have you received forgiveness for?

_____

_____

_____

_____

_____

_____

_____

_____

_____

_____

_____

_____

_____

_____

_____

_____

_____

_____

7. Every family has its own set of special and awkward dynamics. Where do you fit in to your family? Are you able to share and be authentic with your family of origin?

_____

_____

_____

_____

_____

_____

_____

_____

_____

_____

_____

_____

_____

_____

_____

_____

8. Kevin found a way to cope with difficult circumstances through alcohol, but drugs and alcohol aren't the only unhealthy ways people use to hide their true feelings or deal with situations. Did you know that being a chronic people pleaser, food, and even being an overachiever can be an unhealthy way to cope? How do you deal with pain? Has a seemingly healthy habit become an idol in your life?

_____

_____

_____

_____

_____

_____

_____

_____

_____

_____

_____

_____

_____

_____

_____

_____

_____

_____

_____

_____

_____

_____

_____

_____

_____

_____

_____

_____

_____

_____

_____

_____

_____

_____

9. Ephesians 4:31-32 (NLT) says, "Get rid of all bitterness, rage, anger, harsh words, and slander, as well as all types of evil behavior. Instead, be kind to each other, tenderhearted, forgiving one another, just as God through Christ has forgiven you." Are you holding on to anger about things that have happened in your life or with someone?

_____

_____

_____

_____

_____

_____

_____

_____

_____

_____

_____

_____

_____

_____

_____

10. Think about a time when you had to give up your own ideas and plans in order to walk in full obedience to God. Did you receive any resistance from others?

_____

_____

_____

_____

_____

_____

_____

_____

_____

_____

_____

_____

_____

_____

_____

_____

_____

_____

_____

_____

_____

_____

_____

_____

_____

_____

_____

_____

_____

_____

_____

_____

_____

_____

_____

_____

_____

_____

_____

11. ". . . Forgive others, and you will be forgiven," Luke 6:37 (NLT).

Treating your friends with kindness is not tough; but treating others with kindness who are difficult, who you may not like, who are unkind, or rub you wrong is the Jesus way to live. Is there someone in your life who is especially difficult for you to be around? Pray about the situation and ask God for wisdom in how to best show kindness.

QUESTIONS FOR REFLECTION AND DISCUSSION

12. "From his abundance we have all received one gracious blessing after another," John 1:16 (NLT).

Grace Wins EVERYTIME! What does grace look like to you? Have you ever extended grace? Have you ever received grace? How did it change you?

_____

_____

_____

_____

_____

_____

_____

_____

_____

_____

_____

_____

_____

_____

_____

13. Have you been impacted by *Never Give Up?* The authors would love to hear from you. Email them at barkmank@gmail.com.

_____

_____

_____

_____

_____

_____

_____

_____

_____

_____

_____

_____

_____

_____

_____

_____

_____

Grace Wins
EVERYTIME!

About the Authors

Kevin Barker experienced the King of grace and forgiveness in the spring of 2002 and has been passionate about pointing others to their creator ever since. He actively serves with *One Eighty*, an organization that exists to bring hope, love, and opportunity to individuals and communities impacted by crisis, poverty, or addiction. Kevin also joins people from all over the country to build houses in Mexico and Guatemala in short-term missions offered through *Casas Por Cristo*. He resides in Moline, Illinois with his wife, Lynn. Together, they enjoy spending time with friends and family.

Melissa Morse is known by others as someone who loves, serves, and witnesses through hospitality and her giftedness in the creative arts. Her love for her family is undeniable and can be found anytime in her never-give-up spirit for them to have success in faith, love, life, good health, and happiness. Married nearly fifteen years to her favorite hero and best friend, Robert and Melissa have lived all over the US—their favorite being time shared in the Greater Pacific Northwest. As a proud Army wife, Melissa has a special place in her heart for the military community, and has received multiple Gold President's Volunteer Service Awards for the countless hours she has served.

A Note from the writer of
Never Give Up

As a ghostwriter (someone who collaborates with the author of a story and writes it), it is always an honor when someone chooses to share their story with me in a way that I am able to capture it in writing. In order for me to do this effectively, the author needs to openly share details (that may or may not make it in the book) about their story in order for me to truly understand and write from their perspective. This requires authenticity and courage on the part of the author. I never take for granted how difficult this can be and I consider it a true gift to be trusted to write the words of someone's heart and soul.

When I first met with Kevin to discuss his idea for a book, we initially thought that this was a story that Kevin wanted to share. It was both his testimony as well as the story of one of the greatest miracles he had seen God do in his life: restore the relationship with his daughter.

After meeting with Kevin and Melissa both together and separately, it became clear to me that there was more than just one story going on. Their testimonies, unbeknownst to them at the time, overlapped in such a way that I began to see something beautiful in a big-picture kind of way. The more we met, the more it became clear that this wasn't just Kevin's story or Melissa's story, it was a story of how God weaved the two together for a much bigger purpose. Just the act of the two of them sharing, responding and writing it all out was a healing process in itself.

Never Give Up was more than just a writing project for me. God used Kevin and Melissa's story to show me some truths about my own life. How many times have I given up on a dream, a miracle, or just plain old didn't want to hang in there? How many times have I heard or used the phrase, "God's not done with me yet," only to give up on myself, or worse, give up on Him? How many times have I tried to hide from messy situations in a place that was not from God?

I have experienced the pain of people giving up on me. And I have transferred those experiences on to what I thought God must think of me. Afterall, if someone who should love me doesn't, then maybe God doesn't love me either.

I've worked hard for things, fought for relation-ships, and lost heart when the reward did not come.

I have felt like giving up. More than once. I'd be willing to bet that, in some area of our lives, we all have.

As I helped compile and write this book for Kevin and Melissa, it touched me how the miracle wasn't just that their relationship was restored. There were miracles in the everyday obedience when it was hard. There were miracles in forgiveness, both towards others and forgiving themselves. There were miracles in the ownership of baggage and in the setting of boundaries.

Let's be clear; not all relational issues are healed. But I guess that is not really up to me to know how some of my own stories will end. I can only trust that God has a beautiful, big-picture plan in mind that goes far beyond what my expectations are.

This story was a great illustration of that for me.

Robin Grunder, Ghostwriter *Never Give Up*
LegacyPress.org
Robin@legacypress.org

LEGACY press

www.ingramcontent.com/pod-product-compliance
Lightning Source LLC
Chambersburg PA
CBHW021128020426
42331CB00005B/665